How To...

Audio Access Included 🔊

BUILD DRUM GROOVES OVER BASS LINES

BY ALAN ARBER

T0081889

To access audio visit:
www.halleonard.com/mylibrary

"Enter Code"
3938-1285-5445-1710

ISBN 978-1-5400-4335-1

Visit Hal Leonard Online at
www.halleonard.com

Contact us:
Hal Leonard
7777 West Bluemound Road
Milwaukee, WI 53213
Email: info@halleonard.com

In Europe, contact:
Hal Leonard Europe Limited
42 Wigmore Street
Marylebone, London, W1U 2RN
Email: info@halleonardeurope.com

In Australia, contact:
Hal Leonard Australia Pty. Ltd.
4 Lentara Court
Cheltenham, Victoria, 3192 Australia
Email: info@halleonard.com.au

CONTENTS

The mission of *How to Build Drum Grooves Over Bass Lines* is to demonstrate how a drummer and bass player should interact with and respond to each other in different musical styles. Each section of the book presents a bass guitar line in the style of a specific genre, which is then followed by four different drum grooves. These mini-lessons achieve two goals: 1) they illustrate what a drummer should listen for in a bass line, and 2) they demonstrate how to build and execute proper drum grooves.

When I listen to a bass line, I pay special attention to the rhythm the bass player is playing. Each exercise in this book builds a drum groove by orchestrating which drum(s) can be played around that rhythm. You can use each exercise as a building block that leads to the fourth—and final—groove of each section, although each drum example can stand alone and will work perfectly fine with the bass guitar line given.

ABOUT THE AUDIO

To access all of the audio that accompanies this book, simply go to *www.halleonard.com/mylibrary* and enter the code found page on 1. The music examples that include audio are marked with an icon throughout the book.

DRUM LEGEND

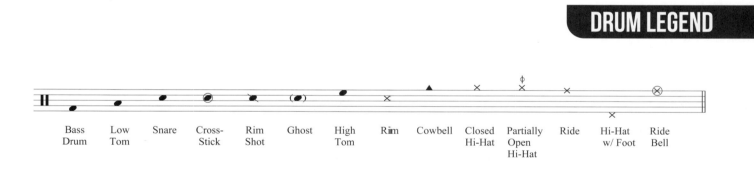

| Bass Drum | Low Tom | Snare | Cross-Stick | Rim Shot | Ghost | High Tom | Rim | Cowbell | Closed Hi-Hat | Partially Open Hi-Hat | Ride | Hi-Hat w/ Foot | Ride Bell |

3

POP ROCK (STRAIGHT 8THS)

♩ = 116

Bass Line

Drum Groove 1

Drum Groove 2

Drum Groove 3

Drum Groove 4

♩ = 76

Bass Line

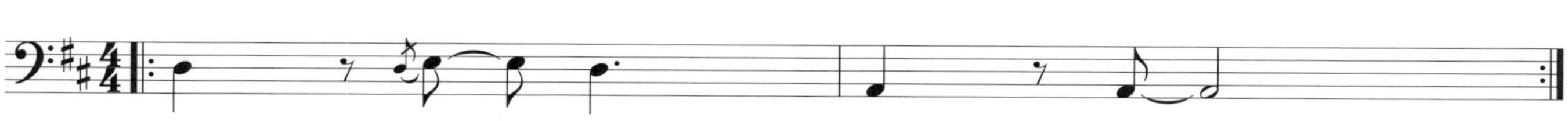

Drum Groove 1

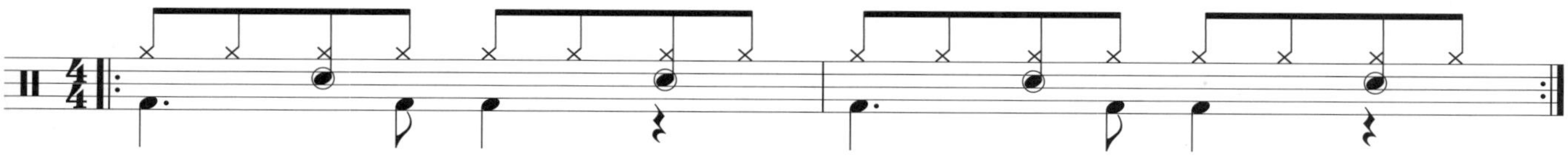

Drum Groove 2

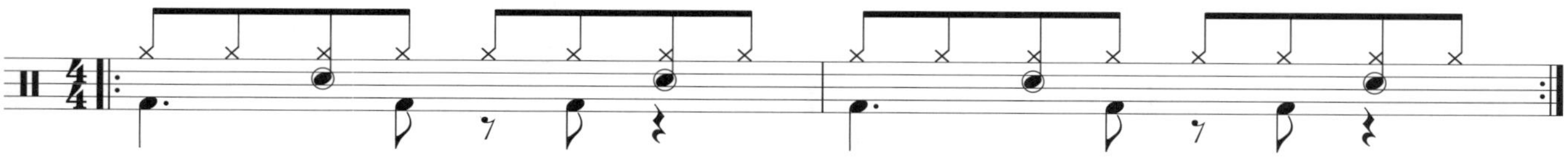

Drum Groove 3

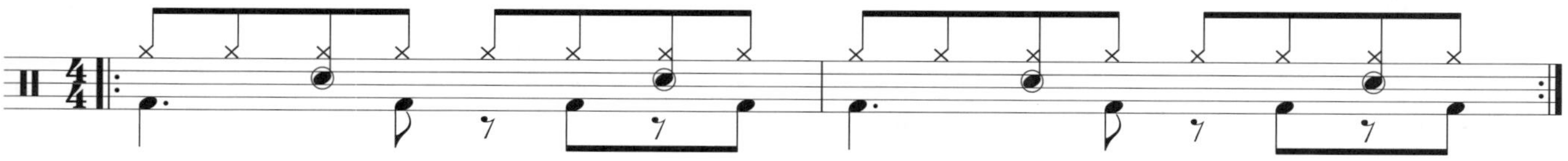

Drum Groove 4

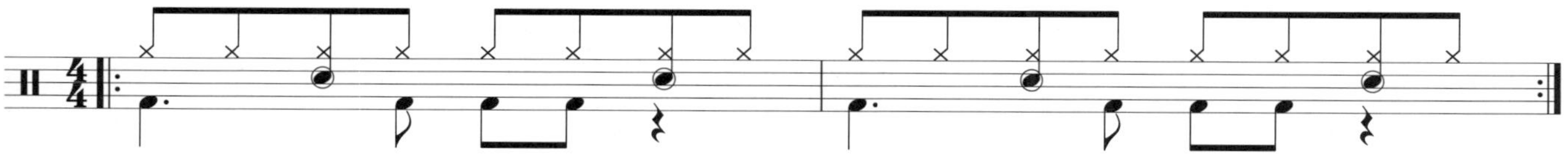

FUNK (STRAIGHT 8THS)

ONE-HANDED 16TH-NOTE FUNK

♩ = 77

Bass Line

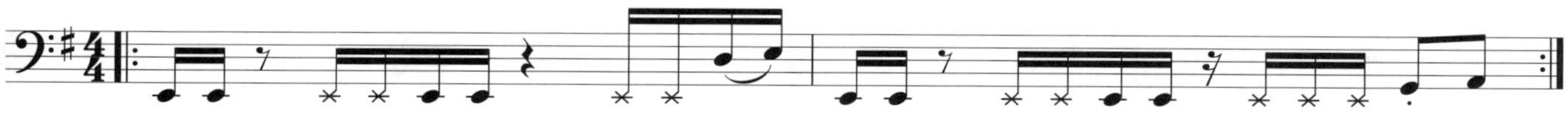

Drum Groove 1

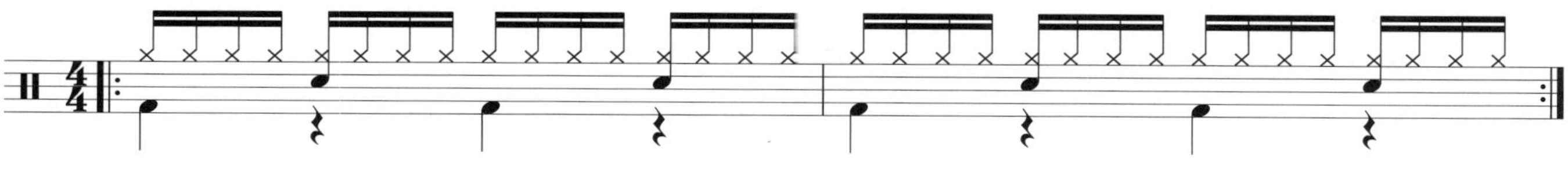

Drum Groove 2

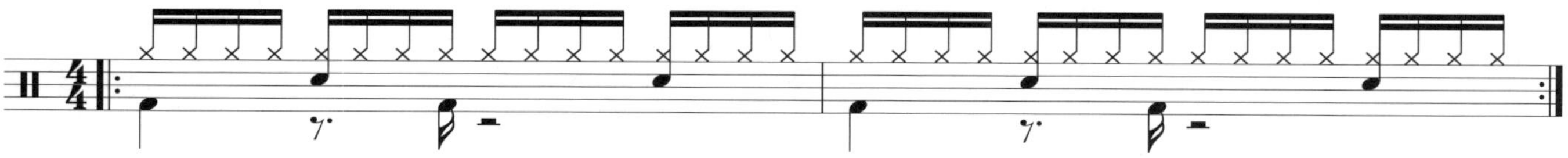

Drum Groove 3

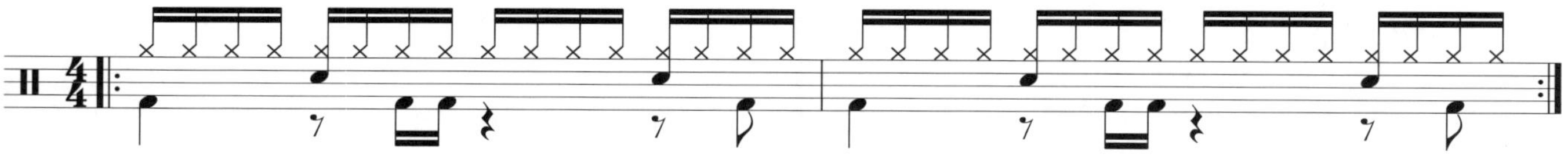

Drum Groove 4

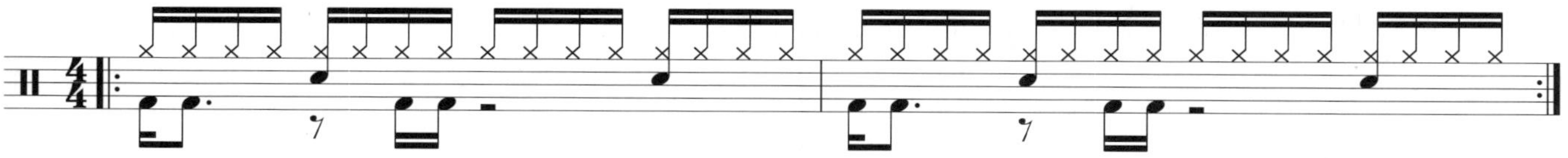

♩ = 83

Bass Line

Drum Groove 1

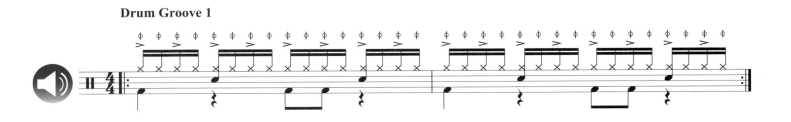

Drum Groove 2

Drum Groove 3

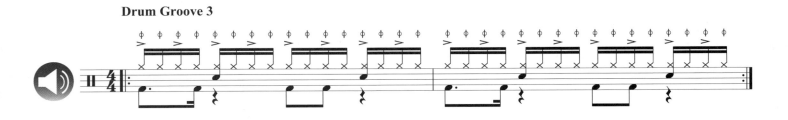

Drum Groove 4

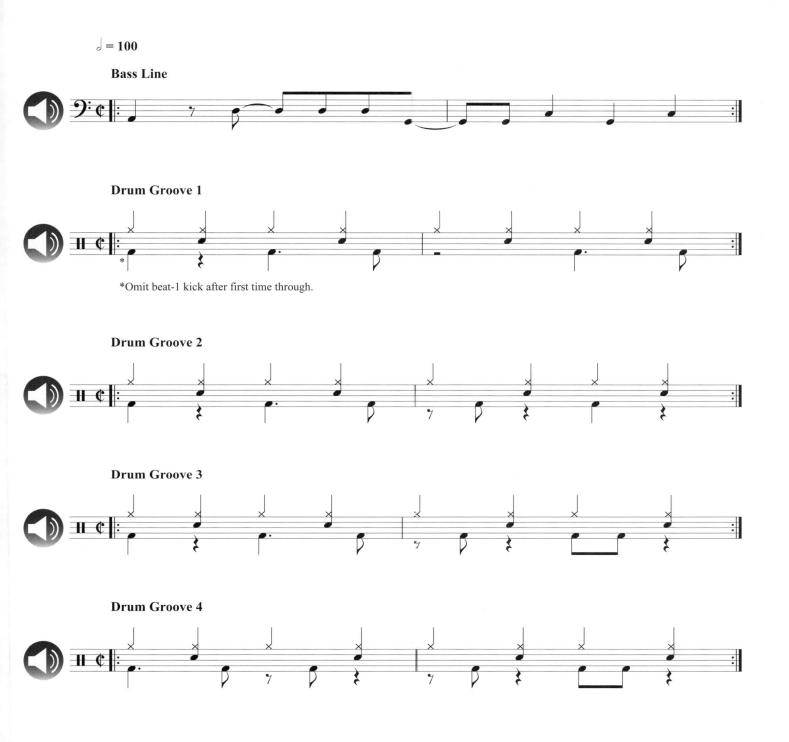

*Omit beat-1 kick after first time through.

TEXAS SHUFFLE

$\quad$ = 112 ($\sqcap$ = $\overset{3}{\sqcap}$)

Bass Line

Drum Groove 1

Drum Groove 2

Drum Groove 3

Drum Groove 4

$\quad \bullet = 150 \ (\sqcap = \overset{3}{\sqcap}\ )$

Bass Line

Drum Groove 1

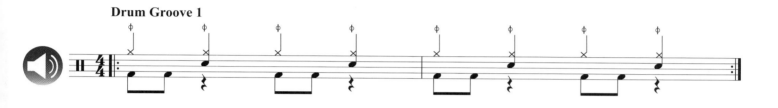

Drum Groove 2

Drum Groove 3

Drum Groove 4

HALF-TIME SHUFFLE

$\quad \bullet = 120 \; (\sqcap = \overset{3}{\sqcap})$

Bass Line

Drum Groove 1

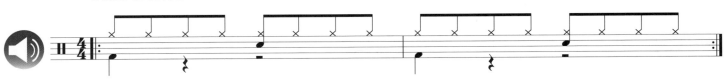

Drum Groove 2

Drum Groove 3

Drum Groove 4

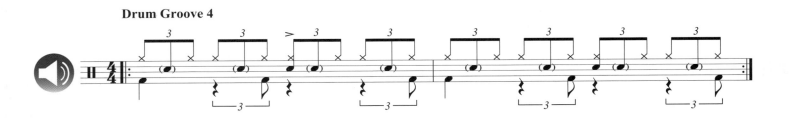

FOUR ON THE SNARE

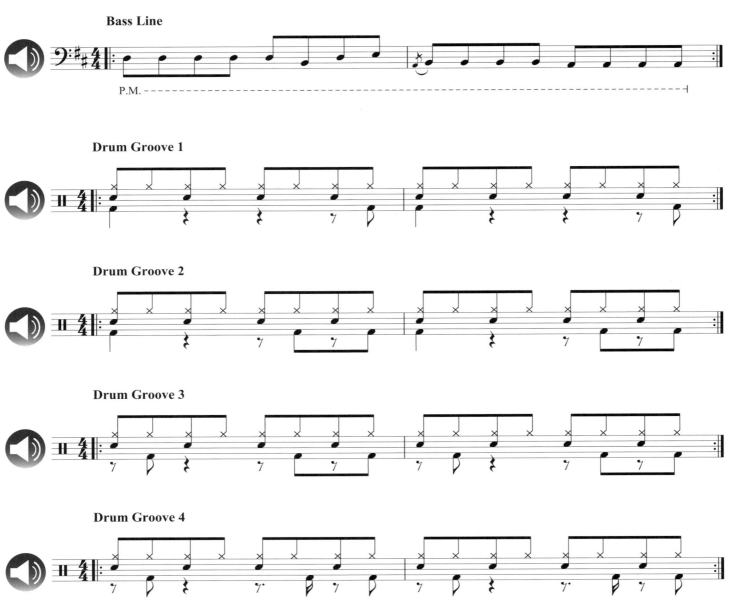

REGGAE

♩ = 70

Bass Line

P.M. -| P.M. -|

Drum Groove 1

*Add optional ghost notes as heard in the recording.

Drum Groove 2

*Add optional ghost notes as heard in the recording.

Drum Groove 3

*Add optional ghost notes as heard in the recording.

Drum Groove 4

*Add optional ghost notes as heard in the recording.

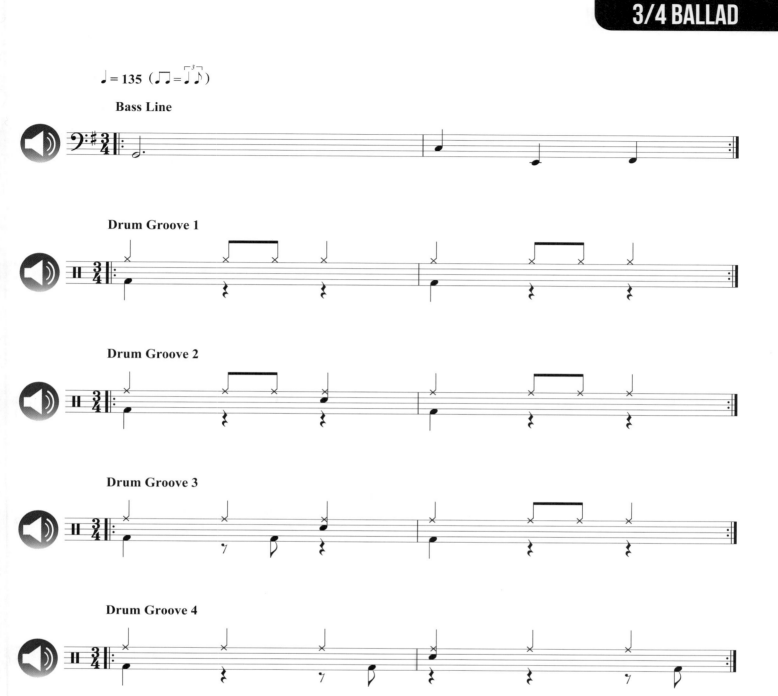

SECOND LINE GROOVE

♩ = 82 (♫ = ♪♪)

Bass Line

Drum Groove 1

Drum Groove 2

Drum Groove 3

Drum Groove 4

♩ = 112

Bass Line

Drum Groove 1

Drum Groove 2

*Add optional ghost notes as heard in the recording.

Drum Groove 3

*Add optional ghost notes as heard in the recording.

Drum Groove 4

*Add optional ghost notes as heard in the recording.

JUNGLE MUSIC (DRUM AND BASS)

♩ = 175

Bass Line

w/ synth effect

Drum Groove 1

Drum Groove 2

Drum Groove 3

Drum Groove 4

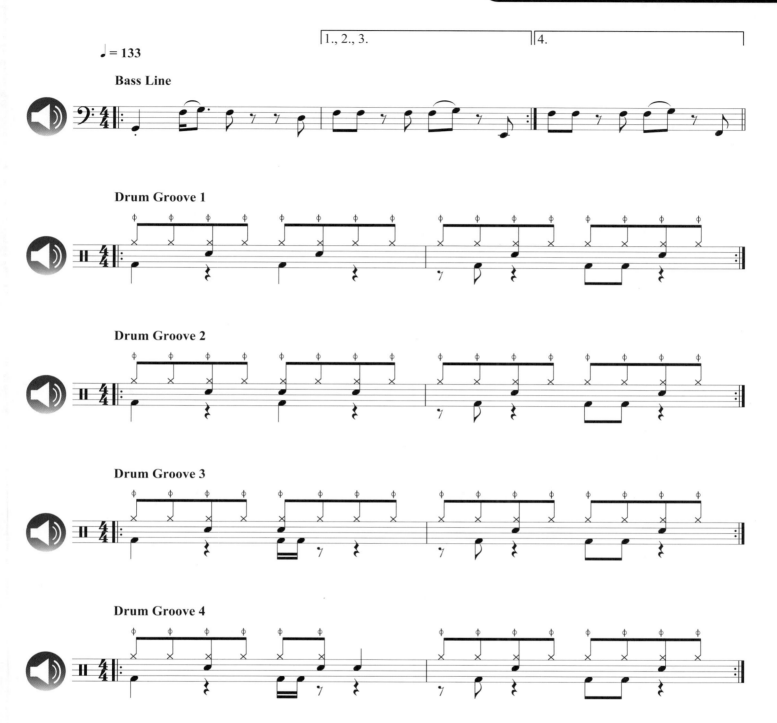

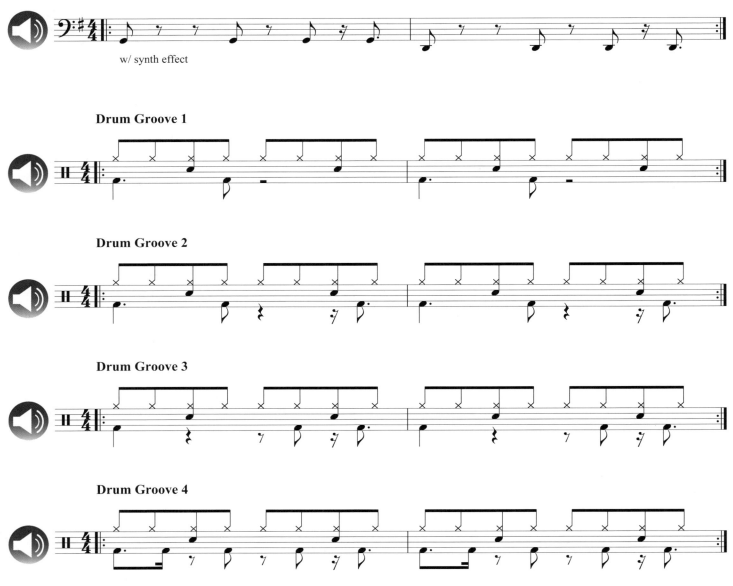

♩ = 90

Bass Line

P.M. - ┤

Drum Groove 1

Drum Groove 2

Drum Groove 3

Drum Groove 4

SLOW HEAVY ROCK

♩ = 66

Bass Line

Drum Groove 1

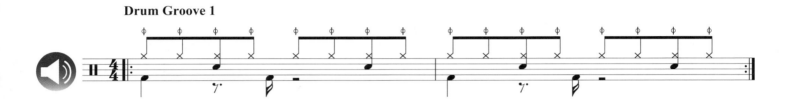

Drum Groove 2

Drum Groove 3

Drum Groove 4

♩. = 117

Bass Line

Drum Groove 1

Drum Groove 2

Drum Groove 3

Drum Groove 4

♩ = 110

1., 2., 3. | 4.

Bass Line

Drum Groove 1

Drum Groove 2

Drum Groove 3

Drum Groove 4

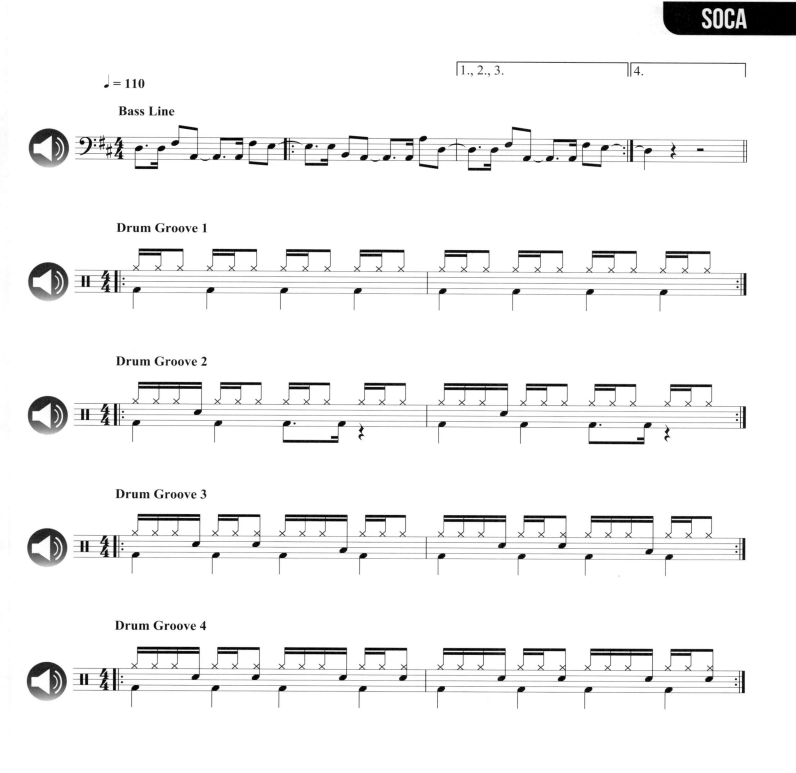

FUNK SAMBA

♩ = 123

Bass Line

Drum Groove 1

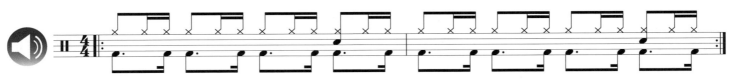

Drum Groove 2

Drum Groove 3

Drum Groove 4

RHUMBA

♩ = 79

Bass Line

Drum Groove 1

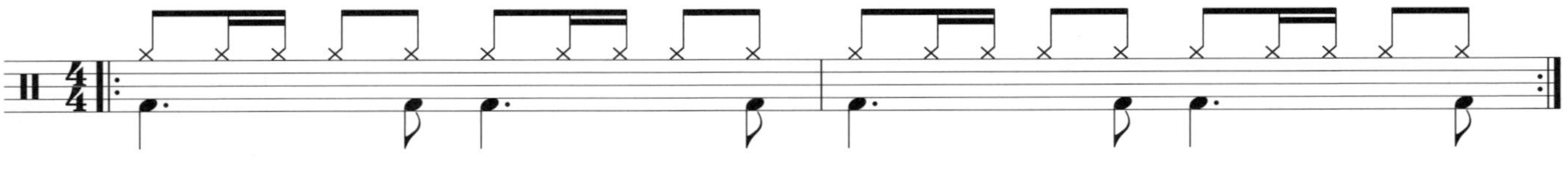

Drum Groove 2

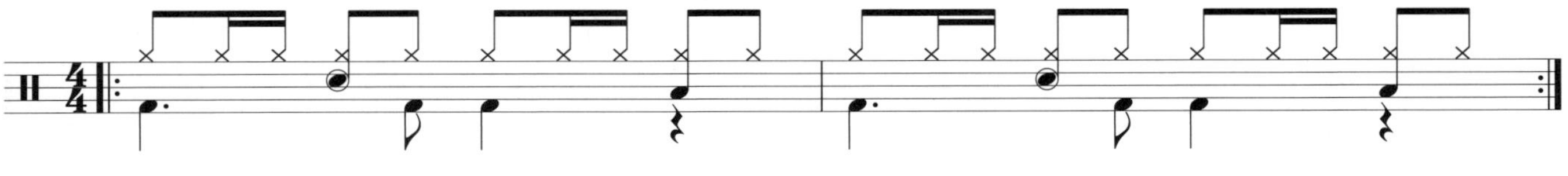

Drum Groove 3

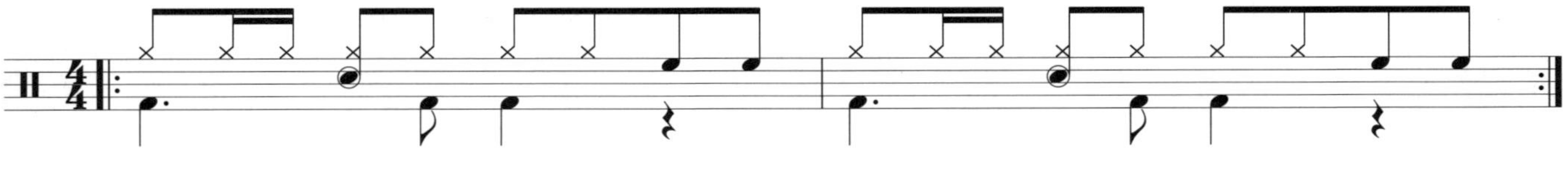

Drum Groove 4

♩ = 165

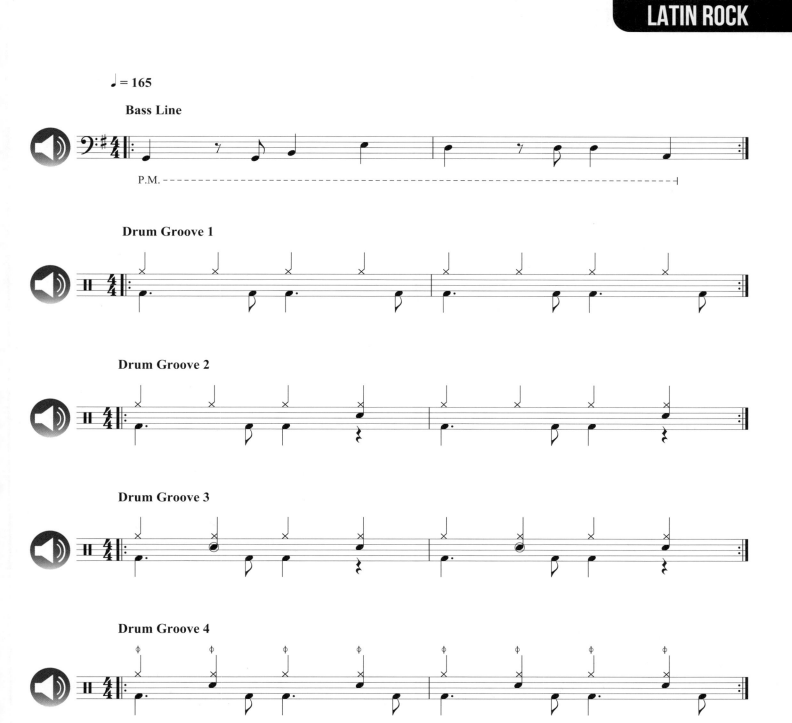

LATIN POP (REGGAETON)

♩ = 100

Bass Line

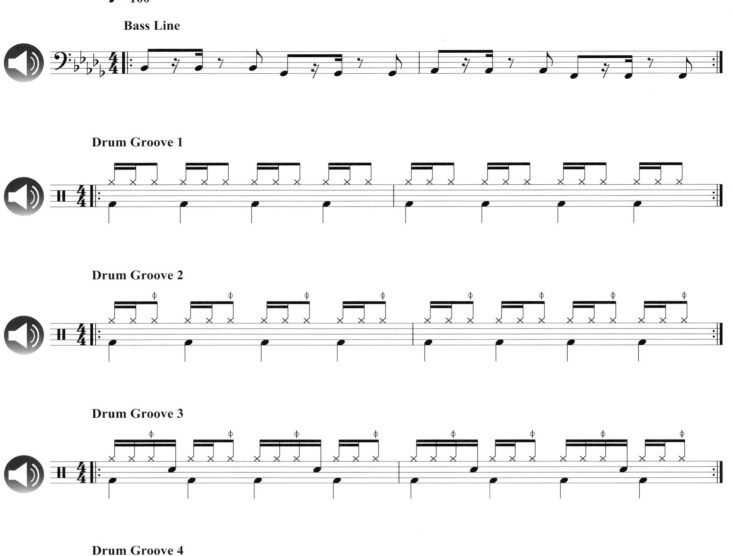

Drum Groove 1

Drum Groove 2

Drum Groove 3

Drum Groove 4

♩ = 116

Bass Line

Drum Groove 1

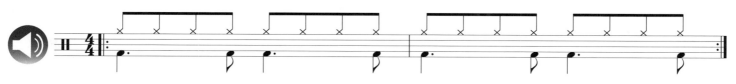

Drum Groove 2

Drum Groove 3

Drum Groove 4

♩ = 88

Bass Line

*Slide 1/2
step above.

P.M.

Drum Groove 1

Drum Groove 2

Drum Groove 3

Drum Groove 4

Play 6 times

BO DIDDLEY BEAT

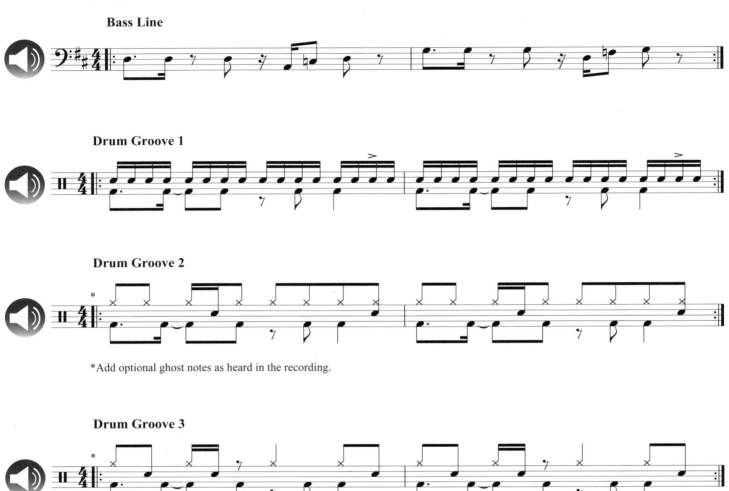

*Add optional ghost notes as heard in the recording.

*Add optional ghost notes as heard in the recording.

*Add optional ghost notes as heard in the recording.

Bass Line

Drum Groove 1

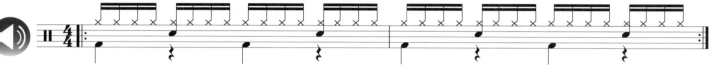

Drum Groove 2

Drum Groove 3

Drum Groove 4

TWO-HANDED 16TH-NOTE GROOVE

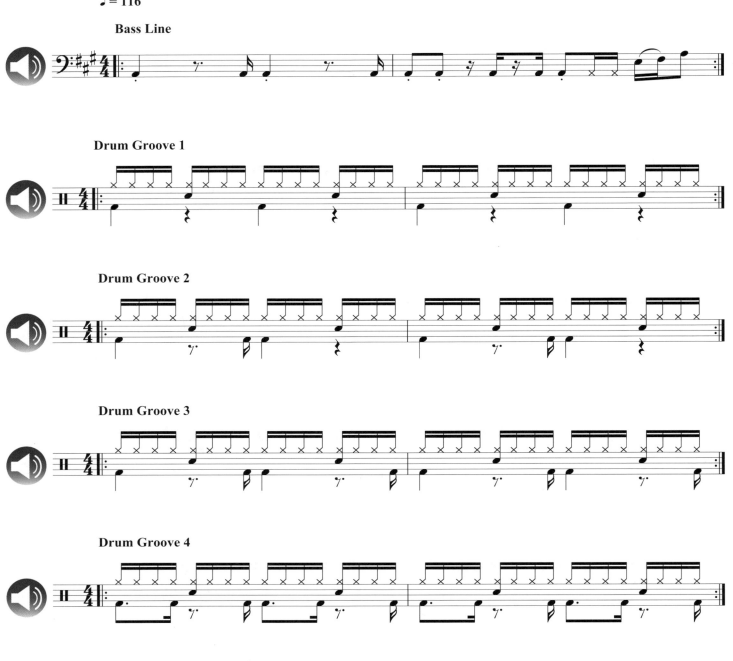

♩ = 87

Bass Line

Drum Groove 1

Drum Groove 2

Drum Groove 3

Drum Groove 4

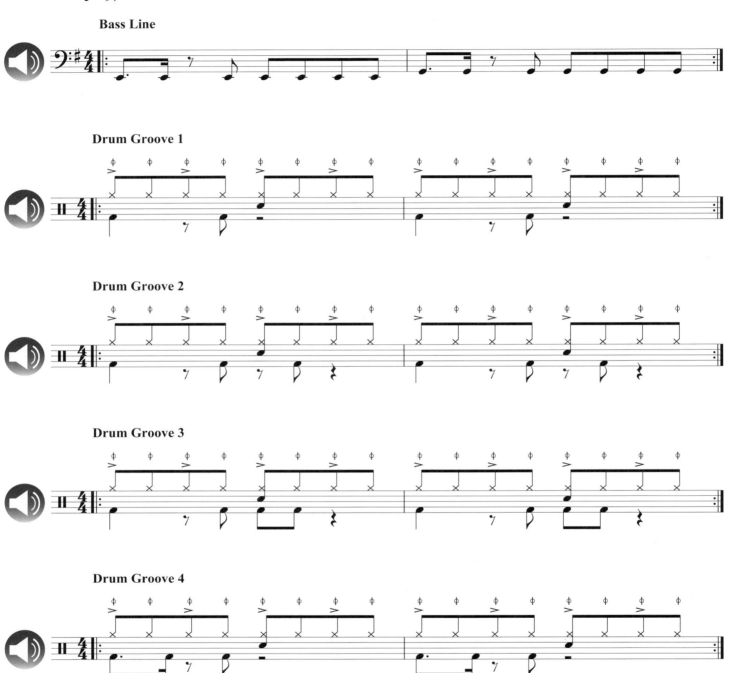

𝅗𝅥 = 119

Bass Line

Drum Groove 1

Drum Groove 2

Drum Groove 3

Drum Groove 4

AFRO-CUBAN FUNK

♩. = 146

Bass Line

Drum Groove 1

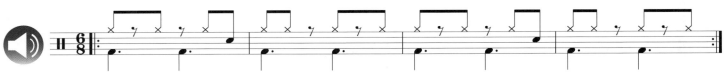

Drum Groove 2

Drum Groove 3

Drum Groove 4